RETAIL READY SECRETS

NEIL AND KAREN GWARTZMAN

Beverly Hills Publishing

*We are where we are because of Paul Gwartzman
and Arnold Stein, two amazing entrepreneurs who
shared with us their insight and experience.*

*Entrepreneurship can be learned, but it's
most potent when inherited.
Thank you for passing along your
most powerful gifts.*

CONTENTS

INTRODUCTION

Imagine walking into a brick-and-mortar store like Walmart, Target, GNC, or PetCo, and you see your product and brand sitting on the shelves. Imagine customers touching and holding it, placing it into their shopping cart, and heading to the check out. What an incredible feeling. The feeling of... You made it!

Although this finish line may seem far away right now, it doesn't have to be. You can start this journey and be one of the millions of brands sitting on a retail brick-and-mortar store shelf. Join us as we share with you how we did it with our Retail Ready Secrets.

So many of our Private Labeling students asked us to write Retail Ready Secrets to help them scale their private label product businesses beyond the boundary of the internet. Yes, scaling beyond Amazon.

In our first book, *Private Label Secrets*, we shared the Private Label Blueprint® by walking the reader through the process of finding a perfect product, putting their brand on the product, and sharing it with millions of customers online.

But building a business doesn't stop there. There are so many other places to share your brand and make an even more significant impact.

Our mission for this book is to share with you a bigger opportunity for product brand success, in retail brick-and-mortar. As you will soon learn more about our background and personal 35-year retail brick-and-mortar journey, we felt that it was important to share our Retail Ready Secrets to encourage you to continue on your journey and go for your dream! We are living proof, dreams come true.

With that being said, if you have a physical product brand and are ready, really ready, to see it grow and impact at a much deeper level, then sit back, relax, and enjoy the read. We are about to share with you the details of how to get your private label product brand "Retail Ready" and on the shelves of your favorite brick-and-mortar stores.

Before we proceed, it is essential to clarify the number one myth around brick and mortar: the myth that brick-and-mortar stores will not survive the rise of e-commerce.

First, brick-and-mortar retail stores are never going away. They will always exist, and online commerce will always exist with it. And, although they continue to compete and fight with each other, equal co-existence is the future.

> Customers still shop in stores today and will continue to do so. Brick-and-mortar stores still play an important role in retailing, with 46% of shoppers saying that they prefer to buy in a physical location. However, 35% prefer buying via laptops and 18% prefer buying via mobile phones, according to the "Shopper-First Retailing" report.

We were just at the mall picking up last-minute school supplies that our kids needed today! As human beings, we need social interaction, and shopping in person in a brick-and-mortar store is one pleasant and popular outing that allows for this interaction.

The stories you hear about stores closing down are not because of online commerce, but more due to other non-related issues like poor marketing, mismanagement, and poor purchasing, to name a few.

Don't get us wrong; yes, online platforms have created a challenge for the brick-and-mortar retailer in the form of competition. The good news is the brick-and-mortar retailers who want to survive and grow are not skulking away with their tails between their legs. They are beginning to take notice of the change in retail and showing hunger and willingness to compete and fight back. To stay ahead of the competition, they're refreshing their images and updating their strategies by being open to adding new brands to their stores to keep their customers from shopping elsewhere. We're already starting to see a balance and co-existence of brick and mortar and e-commerce.

Years ago, retail brick-and-mortar stores were only focused on well-known popular brands and products to fill their shelves, as this brought in foot traffic. Getting products on the retail shelves was tough if you weren't a big name brand.

E-commerce has opened up the opportunity to allow anyone, from anywhere, to sell their private label brands. The popularity around the name of the brand is now not as important as it has been in the past. Now, don't read that last statement incorrectly. What we're saying is brand names that are popular and have built up a reputation are super important to success; however, you don't have to be that super popular brand for a retail brick-and-mortar store to acknowledge your products and want them on their shelves.

In fact, you don't need experience with products or have to be in business for years to get on retail shelves. Many brands that are just starting and have little or no sales are getting on retail shelves. It doesn't matter if your brand is new, you only have one product in your brand-line, or you have only sold a few hundred dollars' worth of inventory. If you have a product that can solve a problem and can prove it's wanted and needed by others, then that product would be a perfect fit for a brick-and-mortar store. So, let's get it on the shelves.

Knowing now that doors are open to a bigger opportunity to retail success, let's jump in and explore a deeper understanding of retail brick and mortar, the tools you'll need, and the step-by-step blueprint for getting your products on the retail shelves.

The process of getting your product on retail shelves doesn't have to be complicated, but you do need to thoroughly understand the process so that it works to your advantage. Let's begin by taking a deeper look at the difference between selling online and selling in brick-and-mortar retail stores.

The massive advantage of retail brick and mortar is, of course, the bigger financial gain as a business, which we will discuss in a bit. I want to first focus here on something a little deeper: the personal feel and immediate gratification the customer receives. These are two super important emotions that drive a brand to success at a deeper, more effective level. Understanding this is important because if this is accomplished, you will see fast and significant success in the brick-and-mortar space.

In brick-and-mortar retail stores, the customer's product experience, which includes seeing, touching, smelling, tasting, and purchasing the product right in the moment is very impactful. That instant gratification is often the deciding factor of success in the retail space. This in-house experience allows the customer to bond and build a connection with your brand and the store from which they are purchasing it on a deeper level than they receive with the online experience.

This is important because this does two things: create loyalty to the brand and create loyalty to the retailer. All of which then affect your brand success in the retail brick-and-mortar space. As well, when your brand is in stores and many stores, your brand can be seen and acknowledged in a way online e-commerce can't compete.

This experience is very different from the one customers receive while online shopping. Online, there seems to be a disconnect when it comes to loyalty. Think about it: When you are shopping online, do you shop by brand or by product? If you shop by brand, then you have likely already experienced the brand, which means you physically touched, smelled, saw, tasted, and/or experienced the products that brand sells at some point in the past. You already created a deep, personal connection to the brand and you shop by brand because of loyalty. Again, loyalty was created by an in-person experience with that brand at some point. When searching online for a product, most search by product category, keywords, or identification of a product, for instance: Cat bed.

> The vast majority (87%) of shoppers begin product searches on digital channels, up from 71% last year.

Although the initial connection starts online, here is where the disconnect is: the mental connection to build loyalty comes from the in-person purchasing experience. The online experience that solidifies the relationship to the brand takes too long and often gets lost along the way. Even with Amazon Prime two-day shipping, the journey from experience and brand loyalty is still too long.

Think about it: When someone shops on Amazon, they

aren't shopping there because they are loyal to your brand. They are connected to the Amazon customer experience. The loyalty they develop is to Amazon and not your brand. That's why is it's so important, if you want to create a strong brand that scales, to nurture loyal customers that you connect with from that first experience.

Remember, too, that loyalty isn't always constant. Even your most devoted advocates need to be reminded of your brand on occasion. Being on retail shelves is a constant reminder that you are a quality brand to remember. It's much harder to bond like that online.

Another great advantage of having your products in retail stores is that you don't sell directly to the consumer, meaning, you don't sell only one product at a time. When you sell to retail brick and mortar, you aren't trading one product at a time in the same way you would directly to a consumer. When selling to a retail store, you are selling your product in larger quantities, such as by the case or palette. What does this mean? It means that you sell more of your product and, as such, your product will reach more customers. The result is a more significant impact and a bigger financial gain.

You must also consider this: When you sell online, you have to work extremely hard on your product's online visibility. On the other hand, brick-and-mortar retail stores already have the profile and customers in place for you.

We're not saying that you shouldn't sell online. There are huge advantages of selling online and we encourage you to continue to do so. What we *are* saying is that you shouldn't ignore the opportunity to get your product and your brand into more hands. Adding other platforms to sell your products will open up many doors and help you scale your business, make more money, and become a leader in your industry. You will not only be able to share your brand with millions of customers, but you will also add a revenue stream to your business. Who doesn't want that?

So, take a moment, close your eyes, and open your mind to the possibility of selling your personal branded products on the shelves of retail stores.

If this sounds amazing to you, you aren't alone. It's totally doable! We have helped many product entrepreneurs get their products into retail stores.

People ask us all the time, "How many products do you have in retail stores?"

We did the math, accounting for over 35 years of developing products for some of the biggest retailers in the world like Walmart, Michaels, and Martha Stewart. We discovered we had personally private-labeled 879 products that made it to the shelves of over 600 retail stores.

Wow, right?

We were shocked, too, even though we've been doing this for three and a half decades. It's no wonder people call us the King and Queen of Products. Our students tell us all the time how grateful they are to be able to learn these secrets from people who love what they do and are still deep in the trenches of retail. This is what sets us apart from anybody else teaching this. In simple terms, we walk our talk.

In this book, we will share with you all the angles of getting your product into retail stores through both perspectives —both as the product pitcher and as the brick-and-mortar store choosing new products. We can do this authoritatively because we have been on both sides of the fence. We have owned numerous brick-and-mortar stores—and still own one—and we have clients pitching to us. We've used that experience over the years to develop the lessons we share with product entrepreneurs who want to break into physical stores.

We understand the dynamics of the retail business from the viewpoint of a buyer and what is required to achieve success. We also have our private-labeled brands. As we mentioned before, our products are, and have been, in over 600 stores around the world in the last 35 years. We know what it's like being on your side, going in, and pitching to stores as well.

We have used our retail-ready process over and over again. We will share what that looks like, so you can be a rockstar when making your pitch. Information with the amount of value, expertise, or strategies we share is rare.

Remember, we grew up in the retail industry. We joke that Neil was born with a barcode on his butt. Neil can think back to the age of ten and remember what it was like working in family businesses that involved retail, manufacturing, and distribution of products. He learned a lot from a young age. He was there at the ground level and watched his family business grow into what it is today. He saw every aspect of the dynamics of this industry.

Again, our knowledge in the business stems not just from

what we learned in school, but from doing it throughout our lives. We've mastered the art of success at trade shows; pitching our products; and selling our products to retailers, distributors, and online. Because we are retailers too, we have mastered the process of picking the perfect product. We know how to evaluate a product and understand what the parameters for making the right choices are.

We eat, sleep, and breathe products. This is our life! It is our greatest passion and mission to help others succeed in bringing their brands to life. Private-label branded products are the future. The retail brick-and-mortar stores understand stocking private label brands will help them in their mission of getting great products in the hands of everyone. Why not *your* private label product?

OUR RECORD OF SUCCESS

What does it feel like for us when we see one of our students go through our program, use our techniques and systems, and become successful at selling their products in retail stores? It feels incredible to know that we've impacted someone's life and business forever. At the same time, we know that we've impacted the consumer by helping you and other entrepreneurs share the power of your products.

It's the same rewarding feeling when you sell a product to a retail store, and you walk into that store to see your product there on display.

One day, we know you'll say, "I remember that day!" I will

never forget that first moment when I saw my first product out on the shelves of Walmart. You think to yourself, "Oh, my God, I did it. I'm someone who's making a difference. Someone is going to buy my product. They are going to appreciate it, and they are going to tell other people." And the best part is watching your products and brand become a household name. It's not about being famous, like a movie star. It's more about being famous like, "Wow, I've done something. I've impacted someone's life. I've made a difference."

We can't wait for you have this experience. We hope you will write to us and let us know about it. Your success is truly the fuel that feeds our souls.

CHAPTER 1
HOW TO GET YOUR PRODUCT INTO RETAIL STORES

PRODUCTS CHANGE THE WORLD

When Alessandro Volta invented the first electric battery in the 1800s, he couldn't have imagined that he had just radicalized the way the world would interact with and conserve energy for the next 219 years to come. Today, our mobile devices are powered by rechargeable batteries, and we're quickly moving toward electric vehicles powered by those batteries! The battery is just one product, and look at the massive impact it's had on the world.

Everyone needs a product. Whether out of necessity or purely for luxury purposes, everyone has a desire to make their life easier, and they achieve this by using products. Everyone also desires the need to save time, money, and energy. No matter who you are, or what your income level is, we all look to make our lives better—and products do just that!

Products help in many different ways and change the quality of living for the better. Can you imagine a world without basic household products like toothpaste, toilet paper, laundry detergents, sugar, etc.? Highly inconvenient, right? What would you do if you needed to cut a piece of cloth and there were no scissors or razors around? Think this way about products, and you'll begin to get the idea of how much products have improved our lives and made everyday tasks easier.

People have intimate relationships with products that change their lives. Strike up a conversation with someone about bikes, regardless of their age, and they'll recall, "Oh, I remember my first bike." Because the bike, a product, gave them freedom, independence, and helped them explore their worlds, they formed a bond with that bicycle.

Products can create an emotional connection due to the positive feeling we get from using them, thus creating a constant need for more products. You can probably recall your first baseball mitt or fish tank and how happy you were to have it at the time. Perhaps you still have it and are keeping it for its sentimental value. That sentiment is a result of the emotional connection you forged with the product.

In 2016, the Tempkin Group discovered that buyers with a positive emotional connection to a brand is 7.1 times more likely to make another purchase.

Beyond that emotional connection, products solve problems. A lot of the products in existence today, like the battery, were created out of the need for the inventor to find a solution to a problem.

The modern locks and keys were invented by Linus Yale, Sr. in 1848. Today, they have been improved and redesigned into various forms and have become a part of our daily lives. Even the latest automated door locks still follow the basic principles of Yale's invention.

What about airplanes, cars, trains, ships, and so on? These products have changed the face of transportation in the world today—and they were created centuries ago. Then, there is the refrigerator, which has changed the way we preserve perishable items and keep them fresh for a long time.

There are numerous examples of products that have changed the way we live. By now, you get the picture and understand how products change and shape the world.

THE EVOLUTION OF PRODUCTS

History offers a multitude of examples of the evolution of various products. Consider the automobile; once an invention of convenience for the wealthy, it has now become a vehicle for mass transportation of people and goods alike.

Beyond an increased use of a product, sometimes products

evolve beyond their originally intended use, for example, the telephone. Developed by Alexander Bell in 1876 as a tool for facilitating long-distance communication between two people, the telephone has since become a multitasking product that transcends its intended use when it was invented. We not only communicate with our mobile phones, we text, take photographs, email for business and personal reasons, maintain our calendars, store documents, play games, surf the internet, get directions, and even track our fitness levels.

In the past, the most common reason for buying a product has been need. Today, however, the story has evolved. The automobile that was once a luxury product is now essential product in people's lives. Make no mistake, some cars are created for luxury purposes like Ferraris, Maseratis, and Bentleys, but the general purpose of a car is convenience.

Businesses are now using products to scale, compete, and build credibility. One of the strategies that we teach is the idea of using products to grow.

The moment you add a product to your business is the point in which you are deepening the connection with your clients and allowing others the opportunity to hear and see, to better experience, you and your brand. At that point, you do so much more than just creating a product; you expand your reach as a business by impacting many more people.

By sharing products, you share your story with your market. You increase your credibility and value as a thought leader by sharing your mission and vision with others to help them in their everyday lives.

In the past, product development was exclusively carried out by big companies. That is no longer the case. As we mentioned, you don't have to be big to swim with the sharks. The steps to creating products and solutions are readily available for anyone interested. And it is access to these steps that we offer you.

If you create a product without the business-building strategies that we teach, you will have succeeded in creating just a product. Our process of becoming retail-ready involves so much more... Product marketing (but not the marketing to which you are accustomed), brand building, relationship development, and so much more. All are part of our secret formula to get your products retail-ready.

THE PRODUCT GRAVEYARD

Do you ever wonder what happened to a product you loved as a kid? Or what happens to a product that didn't make it? They pile up in what we call the Product Graveyard. We'll be honest; we have a bunch of products in that graveyard. When a product goes to the graveyard, it doesn't have to stay there.

Sometimes an early death occurs because of timing; the consumer was just not ready for it. Many times we have resurrected a product from the grave to give it new life and success. We just recently just launched a product that languished in the graveyard for over 10 years, and now it's so popular that we can't keep this product on the shelves.

This often happens with patent ideas and inventions. There

are millions, even hundreds of millions, of patents. Many consist of fantastic products that have never been made, and that's because their creators abandoned them, mostly because they didn't understand the business-building strategies that you're about to learn in this book.

These people have done all the hard work and invented the product, but they lack the skillset and knowledge to manufacture and monetize their product.

There are more patents applied for than there are products successfully brought into the market. There is a graveyard of products with patents attached that were never developed. Eventually, some of those products will be created because someone will resurrect them, improve on them, and find their rightful homes.

Today, your product has a better chance than ever of avoiding the Product Graveyard altogether. We have easier access to the knowledge needed to take an idea, create a product, and share it so that commercialization is a viable option.

YOUR PRODUCTS COME TO LIFE

From experience, we know walking into a store and seeing our products on the shelf is an incredible feeling. You may even reach this incredible milestone simply by doing what you're already doing: selling online.

Many retailers scan the internet in search of products that will fit perfectly into their stores. This recently happened to us.

This is an easier and more effective way for a retail buyer to do their job.

Here's what happened: We were approached by a retail chain store for one of our newer products, which is in the process of becoming retail ready, that we had made available for sale online. They wanted to see if we would be interested in having that product in their stores.

That's why it's so important to have your products online. When you sell online on Amazon, Walmart.com, or other marketplace, you must make sure the product is retail-ready just in case you also get the call. If you are not retail-ready, that opportunity will pass and may never return.

If you've read our first book, *Private Label Secrets: The Fastest Way to FIND and BRAND Your Own Products and Make A TON of Money on AMAZON*, which covers how to find and private label a product, then you know how to ensure your product is retail ready right from the start.

Most people don't do that. They just make their product available on Amazon or another marketplace with no thought about what could come next.

If your product is not ready and a retailer comes calling, you'll have to go back to the beginning…and that's if you're lucky. Most who aren't prepared find they missed the window of opportunity to go big and make their product come alive in every sense.

———

IS YOUR PRODUCT RETAIL READY?

Your current situation probably looks something like:

- You have your products listed and online sales are coming in.
- People are leaving reviews.
- The product is well accepted now, and you want to take it to the next level, to reach more people at a larger volume by getting it into retail stores.

You must now go back to the beginning—back to your product foundation—and assess whether the product is *actually* retail-ready. There's a checklist of things that must be done before you can even get in front of a retailer or a buyer to talk about your product. Because, when you're face to face, it's very much like an audition to pitch your product.

You have only one shot, so:

- Make sure your first impression is spot on. They look at your shoes, your clothes, and your hair.
- Make sure your product is ready for presentation and captivating enough for the pitch you're about to make.
- Ensure your packaging is impeccable. Besides the product being of good quality and doing what it needs to do, the most important thing that retailers will look for is the packaging.

When selling online, many entrepreneurs don't think about packaging. In a retail store, however, the packaging is your first —and maybe only—chance to make a good impression.

What does the package look like? What does it say? What does it do? Are you abiding by all the legal specifications on the packaging for the country in which you are selling?

The packaging engages the buyer or retailer with your product through its story and connection that story makes. If your packaging doesn't tell that story, then decision-makers never have that connection and can't develop a relationship with your products.

And you will lose the retail opportunity.

Make sure you can check off the following before you approach a retailer. Keep in mind this is a general checklist, so you should feel free to add items to personalize your experience.

CHECKLIST

1. PRODUCT PURCHASED AT THE LOWEST POSSIBLE PRICE FROM THE MANUFACTURER.
2. PRODUCTION VOLUMES AND SHIPPING FAST AND EFFECTIVE (NO HOLD UPS).
3. PACKAGING RETAIL READY FOR THE SPECIFIC STORES YOU PITCH TO.
4. LINE SHEET COMPLETED.
5. TERMS AND CONDITIONS AND CONTRACTS.

6. ADVERTISING STRATEGY BUDGET IN PLACE.

7. VERBAL PITCH PERFECTED.

8. SHIPPING AND LOGISTICS SET.

9. DISCOUNT AND REBATE STRUCTURE IN PLACE.

10. LIST OF RETAILERS PERFECT FOR YOUR PRODUCT.

CHAPTER 2
PICKING THE RIGHT RETAIL
STORE FOR YOUR PRODUCT

I n this chapter, we'll discuss the importance of selecting the right retail store for your product and the negative consequences that occur when you choose poorly.

When you search for a retailer for your product, you will have countless options to from which to choose. You might think having so many possibilities would make your decision easier, but the truth is that it won't. A wealth of choices can make subtle distinctions in quality more difficult to determine.

When too many choices paralyze you, there's often a greater possibility that you'll end up making the wrong choice. It's easy to pick the best from one or two options, but when the possibilities are virtually endless, you can easily lose your way. You can't afford to choose the wrong retail store. Putting your product in a store where it doesn't perform can be detrimental to your business and immediately send your product to the Product Graveyard.

Those in the music industry understand how the choice of which record label artists sign with can impact a career. There have been many well-publicized cases of musical acts suffering serious setbacks after signing with the wrong company. On the other side are success stories stemming from the right partnership between musician and label, where the executive and representatives understand exactly how to market the act.

Having been in the retail sector for many years, we understand how the wrong store choice can negatively affect your product's potential. Demographics are an important consideration. The right retail store allows you to be confident that your product will be presented to the right consumers. It also helps maximize your exposure and improve your chances of effective sales.

Now that we've highlighted the potential impact retail stores can have on your product, we'll discuss exactly which factors you should consider when choosing a retail store for your product.

If you have a high-end, specialized, and expensive product, your aim should target stores that will emphasize and support the value of that product. However, if you don't properly research your decision and approach a retail store where most customers are bargain shoppers, your product might gather dust on their shelves.

Lesson: It doesn't matter how useful your product is. If your selling price is significantly above the average in its category in a particular retail store, there may be low demand from customers—something a retailer never wants to see.

Another factor to consider when selecting a retail store is the size of your company. This could determine your chances of success with some retail stores. Some of the bigger, more pretentious retailers feel the smaller you are, the less experience you have, which means the inability to keep up with their demands. The stigma they label you with may determine your future success with them.

One of our past clients, we'll call him Mark, lost an opportunity because of this. Mark's company made specialized fabric paints. His product was incredible, and he knew it. Unfortunately, he was a little too confident with his product and he only wanted to see it in the *huge* retail chain stores.

To get the attention of the big retail stores, he went to a trade show where bigger chain stores often attended in hopes of catching their attention. He only wanted to focus on the big guys and showed no interest in any other retailers. To his amazement, these large retail stores ignored him because they considered his company too small to handle their demand. They weren't far off in their assumptions, either. Mark was making the product in his garage and couldn't supply in large quantities. Because of this, the chain stores at the show didn't think he could service their market base.

We met with Mark and shared with him our trade show strategies, explaining that the demand of the huge retailers needs to be met even before you pitch to them. There is a process—steps that need to be completed when first starting out before you get in front of the big guys.

For example, start with the independent retailers as they are often eager to take on new products, regardless of company size. Baby steps are super important in building a global retail brick-and-mortar brand.

After Mark followed our advice, he started gathering momentum. His brand is now sold in some of the largest chain stores in the world: Walmart, Joann Fabrics, and Michaels. He later sold his company for millions and became a recognized leader in his industry.

Lesson: Because he didn't do his research, Mark thought the big chains would jump at his product. Instead, he had to build with smaller retailers, gain credibility, and then expand his company before getting noticed by the big retail stores.

Research is *so* important. Make sure your product is a good fit and you are ready to take on the demands of the retailer. Starting with smaller companies and not jumping in too quickly is the key. When most people think of retailers, they imagine established chain stores like Walmart, Target, and Hobby Lobby: top of the line retailers. However, with increased size come bigger contracts and even bigger demands. This is why we always suggest that our clients start with the independent stores. We encourage them to get their feet wet, learn the process, and then proceed from there. Eventually, when the top retailers come with huge demands, ready to take your product, you'll be ready for them.

Consider these two steps when deciding the best fit retail stores for your product:

(a) Make a list of the retailers in your area that you'd like to sell to. You can also think big and make a list of major retailers as well. You might not start with them when executing your search for the reasons we've discussed, but you can always go back to them later.

(b) Visit the stores you have listed, in person, to see if your product is a good fit. It is not a guessing game.

You'd be surprised at the results these two steps can produce. You must start your journey thinking locally. It will be much easier to serve your market if you're within close proximity to the stores that have your products. You can visit them and promote your product in person, see the sales firsthand and interact with the customers who will love your personal approach.

Another route, already briefly mentioned above, is getting your product into stores by attending trade shows in your city, other states, or even internationally. It doesn't matter where the shows take place. Attend several trade shows and look at products that are similar to your own. Note where the product owners sell their products and who their customers are. In effect, you take advantage of their research for your own purposes. To learn more about trade show success, visit our website at privatelabeluniversity.com

Clients sometimes ask about producing a unique product, unlike any other in the market. Do they still go through the process of attending trade shows? One couple developed a product that was, in their words, "in its own category." While the product was somewhat unique, it was still within a well-established industry in the retail world.

If your product is new and innovative, trade shows are imperative to get your brand and idea visible and understood. Some specialty trade shows focus on new inventions and products, while many general trade shows exhibit new products and have a special area to highlight them.

Keep in mind, a unique product is a much easier sell than one similar to others on the market. You can sell it on its distinctive qualities rather than making an argument as to why it's better than nearly identical products already on the shelves. But you won't sell anything without exposure and education. If the product is a new concept, show and tell will be crucial. Trade shows allow just for that.

Earlier, we advised making a list of retail stores you've researched and would like to approach with your product. Although it is natural to have a favorite retail store on the list, we always recommend that you make your list as extensive as possible and avoid putting all your hopes in one place. That way, if you get rejected by your preferred store, you'll be able to fall back on other options.

If you're not sure where to start with your search, here are some tips that could help.

TIPS

1. SOCIAL MEDIA: Facebook, Instagram and LinkedIn are great resources to find buyers and retailers you can connect to.
2. GOOGLE SEARCH: Do a very defined search on Google and you will find amazing connections.
3. TRADE SHOWS: You can spot buyers in seconds at shows. Interacting with them and knowing what to say is key and advantageous to your brand success.

THE BIG QUESTION: HOW MUCH WILL I NEED TO INVEST?

Even if you've done your research and determined the type of stores you'd like to target, you must be prepared to deal with the question of money. Clients often ask us questions like, "How much is this going to cost?" or "How much money must I invest?" If you aren't able to answer these questions, retailers will assume you're not ready for their stores.

Thinking big means growing your company big, and that involves making bigger investments and commitments to other businesses. If this scares you then congratulations! You're already thinking big.

If these types of commitments are not appealing, then staying small might be right for you. And there's nothing wrong with that. Playing big means bigger results, opening the doors to a much bigger future, but it comes with upfront costs. We share with you the importance of these upfront costs so you will understand the investment that is required when going big with retail distribution.

An interested retailer may come to you in with a forecast or an actual purchase order and say, "I need X number of units to service one hundred chain locations."

Based on this, you can do the math. Maybe what he's asking for is a lot more than you have budgeted. You know that, if you don't have sufficient cash flow to fulfill the retailer's requested quota, you'll lose the contract or they may revoke their purchase order. At this point, you naturally wonder where the money to fulfill the store's order will come from.

Let's assume you receive an order from Walmart, and you need to deliver a hundred thousand dollars' worth of inventory by a certain time to service them. If you don't have sufficient funds to pay for the goods, especially if they're coming from overseas, where you must pay before delivery, you'll be unable to fulfill the order. This is where the importance of cash flow comes into play.

There are methods you can use to establish cash flow, borrow money without penalty, and procure money which can then be reinvested into your products. Any product owner who has no money can use these strategies, techniques, resources, and connections to access cash flow.

If you don't have the cash flow, then you can't fulfill the chain store's order. If you can't fulfill their order, then you won't be able to work with them. This brings us back to our recommendation from earlier: Start with smaller chains.

With smaller chain stores, you can plan and build. You can profit from sales, reinvest, then build up more inventory. With this inventory in place, you can make projections and speculations.

For instance, you might say, "This store has ten locations and they sell this quantity of my product. If I sold on a bigger scale with a store that has fifty locations, I should have this amount of inventory."

In this way, you can develop your strategy as well as a formula determining how much inventory you should have on hand or ready to ship when you're ready for the large retail stores.

It's important to exercise intelligence, research, and foresight as you attempt to bring your product to retailers. Studies have shown that between eighty-five and ninety-five percent of new consumer products fail. At the same time, there is a value on innovation.

> Eighty-three percent of consumers indicate a willingness to pay more for innovative products, and an impressive ninety-three percent of executives agreed that growth through innovation was important to the continued success of their businesses.

What this adds up to is that new products are valued, but it is a competitive market. It will be very important to always work on the latest and trending product. There is no room for mistakes when getting your product on the shelves. You need to proceed wisely and thoughtfully at every step of your journey.

A good case study in approaching retailers is the story of Wolfgang Puck, now a world-famous chef behind a business that grew from his initial forays into restaurants to include an empire of retail products.

Puck started with nothing. He grew up in Austria where his father was a coal miner and part-time boxer, and his mother was a hotel chef. At fourteen, he dropped out of school to be an apprentice chef at the hotel. Later, he studied in France and then worked his way up as a restaurateur in Los Angeles, eventually opening the world-famous Spago. This led first to moving into the frozen food market with a line of frozen pizzas sold locally at the Gelson's chain in Southern California. Sure, he was well known, but he still wisely started locally where he could manage his growth.

Once he had established his foothold, Puck aimed for the national market and expanded beyond consumer packaged goods. For him, that meant avenues of merchandising where he could reach the largest number of consumers across the country simultaneously.

Puck made a deal with QVC and expanded to selling other retail products, such as cookware, knives, and cookbooks. He used the cable shopping network to build interest in his retail products but eventually felt like he could find a better deal.

He jumped ship and signed with QVC's main competitor, the Home Shopping Network. To maintain his prominence on HSN, Puck flew to Tampa six times each year to perform a grueling sixteen hours of live salesmanship in front of the network's cameras. It paid off. Puck noted that this kind of merchandising is where he made the most profit with the least overall effort, noting that he needed over a thousand people to keep his restaurants running, while the entirety of his HSN retail empire only required twenty people to fulfill. It became a sixty million dollar business.

He's a great case study because he followed our suggestions. He started small in retail, selling frozen pizzas on the local market, building his brand recognition before moving to a major nationwide market with nonexpendable goods once he had reached the point that his business and reputation could sustain it.

These steps worked for Wolfgang Puck, and they'll work for you, too. We can testify to this because we've seen the success happen.

Let's look at another case study. Scott was a client of ours who followed the steps previously outlined and met with huge success.

Scott had an amazing product and, initially, didn't carry out the necessary research. He was mesmerized by the idea of seeing his product on the retail shelves and sharpened his focus only on the big A-list stores. Scott wanted to jump right in at the deep end. In his mind, he had a predetermined category (kitchen) where he felt his product would fit. That was his vision, and he was confident that was where it should be.

Because Scott hadn't worked with us from the very beginning, he didn't know how to carry out in-depth research. He didn't understand where his product should be selling, or what category or part of the store it should be selling in. He, on his own, had approached some retailers and had been rejected every single time. Then he came to us.

We took his case and did some tweaking, guiding him back to the drawing board to perform the necessary research. He did as instructed and, in the process, we discovered that the particular category where he originally placed his product was not servicing the right people when they came into the store.

On our advice, he moved the product from the "kitchen" to the "automotive" category, incorporated it into the brand, and turned it into a selling point.

The product wasn't even unique, but he made changes that made it unique to him and his brand. It had been a household product that most people would have assumed was only useful in the kitchen, but in reframing it, he changed their mindset. With just a little tweak on its usage, he turned it into something different. Now people who buy this product use it in their garage and the automotive industry.

When he returned and pitched it to the retailers as something completely different, this time they gladly took it in.

TIPS

1. DO YOUR RESEARCH!
2. PURSUE BUSINESSES THAT HAVE THE RIGHT DEMOGRAPHIC AND PRICE POINT FOR YOUR PRODUCT.
3. LOOK FOR SMALLER LOCAL STORES TO START WITH.
4. CONSIDER WHETHER TWEAKING YOUR PRODUCT OR REFRAMING IT IN A DIFFERENT DEPARTMENT MIGHT MAKE IT MORE SELLABLE.
5. CONSIDER WHAT SETS YOUR PRODUCT APART.
6. BUILD YOUR BUSINESS AS YOU EXPAND TO BIGGER MARKETS.
7. DON'T GET YOUR HEART SET ON A TOP RETAILER AT THE BEGINNING.
8. CONSIDER AND PROJECT THE AMOUNT OF INVESTMENT YOU WILL NEED BASED ON THE RETAILER YOU SHOW YOUR PRODUCTS TO.

At this point, you should have a strong foundation with which to plan your approach to retailers. You must recognize the importance of proper research to focus your search. The margin is pretty fine, and doing your research could be the determining factor between getting your product into the right stores or having it ultimately go nowhere.

Remember that you're looking for a perfect partnership that benefits both parties. Not everybody is a perfect fit with Walmart. They do one kind of thing and do it very well. But your goal isn't to shoehorn your product into the Walmart business plan; it's to find that perfect partner for your product. When you do, it's like puzzle pieces fitting together, and both product and retailer are elevated.

After all the time, work, thought, and passion you've put into developing your product, you can't afford to waste it on the wrong retailer. It's analogous to a romantic relationship: you don't want to pick the first person you see, and you don't want to talk yourself into someone who is appealing on the surface but has nothing in common with you. Wait for your soul mate, that person who completes you. It's the same kind of dynamic with retailers, and when you find it, you can rest assured that product and retailer will prosper together.

CHAPTER 3
PITCHING YOUR PRODUCT

W e've established the importance of finding the right retailer, but it's important to note that this is only half the battle. You also have to convince them that your product will fulfill an important need for their company. This is done with…the pitch!

What is pitching? Simply put, a pitch is a presentation you make when you meet a potential business or client. It's commonplace, and most preferable, for a pitch to be done face-to-face, although you can also initiate the meeting via email or phone call.

Your pitch presents an overview of your company, brand, and product. Explain who you are, why you're meeting, what you can do for their company, what your product is about, and how it can change people's lives—all in only five to ten minutes. That's all the time you'll get to make a lasting impression. Unless you've invented the next hula hoop, everything rides on the pitch.

Naturally, you'd think anyone giving a pitch would already know their product and be ready to present the details: what they're selling, its benefits, and every important characteristic of the product.

This is not always the case.

People sometimes forget to cover all areas. Poor preparation is the worst—and yet most common—pitching mistake a person can make. Poor preparation effectively translates as you not knowing your product and brand as well as you should.

You may think you understand your brand well enough to talk about, but then the questions come rolling in:

- What do you do?
- What's your brand about?
- What does your company do?
- Why should we pursue a relationship with your company?
- What distinguishes your product from others on the market?

These questions will come rapidly, and if you don't sufficiently prepare, you will inevitably fumble. Why? Because you don't know your story.

What *is* your story? What's your brand about? Are you breathing it? Are you living it?

When you answer these questions from someone who knows nothing about you or your brand, you must be able to express yourself on an emotional level.

Before you can sell your product, you must first sell your brand vision. If you can't accurately convey these, you'll never get the chance to even mention your product. Start with a brief story. What prompted you to develop the product? What happened in your life to reveal the need—the pain point—that your product solves? Next, explain why solving this particular need was so important to you. This is your mission—your brand's reason for existing. Then, tell the retailer what sets you and your product apart from any similar brands or products in their stores.

It's heartbreaking when people aren't prepared for their pitch after spending so much time getting their products ready and determining where to sell them. If they're not prepared for the pitch, they may lose an opportunity they'll never have again.

The pitch is not just a verbal exchange along the lines of, "We're company X and here's our product. It would be great in your store." The pitch is a process that takes time to develop.

It is very much like an artist's portfolio. You need to have things ready to show: research already completed, stats calculated, and practical examples. You must be able to tell them how your product works eloquently. Everything needs to be created in this portfolio so that you are prepared when you walk in to meet the retailers. When you're prepared, nothing will stump you.

Your appearance, including your clothing, is an extension of your pitch. In other words, how you present yourself can make or break your pitch. If you're selling some type of mechanical instrument and you walk into the meeting in flip-flops and shorts with messy hair, your potential clients won't take you very seriously. What if, however, you're selling a new swim line and walk in wearing the same flip-flops and shorts? When you then explain, "I live on the beach, and I designed this product. We are lifestyle beachwear and our brand represents comfort on the beach," your clothing becomes something different entirely. Why? Because your outfit matches the pitch you're making.

Essentially, by making sure everything about you (as it is presented to your client) is an extension of your company entitlement, you will be "living the brand." This is a process we help our clients with—bringing their brand and their story together and building their portfolio.

At Private Label University, we prepare you for success by helping you navigate this brand expression. We do this meticulously, paying attention to the smallest detail to guarantee that you are well-prepared. We cover what to wear, what to say about each product, the individual topics to cover, how much time to allot to each subject, what hand gestures to use, which handouts and PDFs to distribute, and much more.

Basically, we help you develop and rehearse every detail that goes into the pitch. We cover all of this with training sessions and templates on what will likely happen before you even get in front of the retailer, including emails, communications, and follow-ups. It's a step-by-step process.

Once you're ready, it's time to initiate contact with your target retailers. It's often difficult to connect with people on the phone. Sometimes you will go through a whole line of people just to reach the person you want to speak to. For this reason, it's easier to get the conversation started with an email.

With the first few emails, you introduce yourself, your product, and what you can do for them. That is ultimately what it's all about: how you can help the retailer make money. If you're successful, your email conversation will lead to a telephone conversation and then to a full-blown face-to-face meeting.

A word of warning: Having thick skin is important. You'll hear the word "no" a lot. Be prepared for rejection. This applies to every step of the process, from the emails, to the phone calls, to the in-person pitch. You're not the only one trying to set up a meeting with them. Retailers get bombarded with emails and usually just skim through most of them.

Persistence is important, but creativity is key. If you're creative with your email messaging, your name and email address will become more recognizable, and the retailer might open them to see what you're saying. Just like that, the "no" may turn to a "YES."

Just be careful. Persistence can easily cross the line into

annoyance. Too many emails might put you on a retailer's blacklist.

When you get to the level where they become intrigued, they'll think, "Who is this person? Let me look her up. Let me check on LinkedIn. Let me check on Facebook and their website." When they do so, they may think, "Wow, this person has a quality product that's being sold in stores. We should probably take a look at it."

If you don't have LinkedIn or Facebook profiles, you could miss out yet again. Establish a social media presence early, including a website that highlights your products along with comments, reviews, and testimonials.

Your personal profile on these platforms isn't enough. You must set up business pages—interactive social media page are even better. Some people just put up their page, and don't do anything with it, but engaging with your audience is extremely important.

LinkedIn is an extremely useful resource for when you're looking for contact information. It is free to use, so there's no reason not to create an account to help connect with buyers or owners of retail stores. Many retailers will ask for this; they want to see an active social media presence.

Keep in mind that email is only one way of starting the pitching process. You might also meet the buyer, the buying group, or the owner at a trade show. Wherever you get your chance, talk to them. Whether you're the exhibitor, or you're walking the show and meeting people, you should be ready to initiate contact and set up a meeting right then and there.

Many ask if we recommend that people keep a spreadsheet of prospects they're connecting with so they can track them and follow up. Focus and organization should be paramount, so yes.

Being focused and organized does not mean, "I'm going to pick five people, and I'm going to be in five stores." It doesn't work like that. You need to make sure your process is organized.

Keep a list of the stores who've rejected you, because "no" doesn't mean "no" forever. No might be, "Call back in a month." It might mean, "This is not the season. Keep us on deck and try later." Keep notes about who you spoke to, when you spoke to them, and exactly what they said. Later, you can reference previous conversations when communicating through email, telephone, or in person.

Detailed organization like this is vital when dealing with chain stores that have so many corporate levels. They may have offices on the East Coast while another part, designated for buying a certain product, is located on the West Coast. At this level, you must be organized—the departments you're contacting, the level of management you're speaking to, and the part of the country where the offices you're speaking to are located.

When your organization is as detailed as this, you can make references like, "I spoke to Janine in this department. She told me to speak to Mr. Anderson on the West Coast, and he handles these separate product lines." This way, you always have your story straight because you know who you're speaking to while you build your map of the people involved in the organization.

If you attend a trade show or retail-focused event and see a retailer's name that you know from LinkedIn, you can easily walk up and engage them. For instance, "Mr. Anderson, I sent you an email. My name is John Smith." By doing this, you can build your contacts, increasing your chances of getting your product into their stores.

Another advantage to this approach is that it gives you information you can ultimately include in your pitch.

"I spoke to Mr. Anderson at a trade show recently..."

You'll have the advantage of a personal touch, giving your audience the impression that you've been there, and you know what and who you're talking about.

It's all about details; get as much detail as you can put down and then organize it. For example, "I sent a sample to Mr. Anderson, but Sam and Jill didn't get the sample." In addition to being material to help you with your pitch, your customer relationship management also helps you keep track of everyone you've engaged with in the past.

When you're speaking to so many people, it's exciting. You may able to remember everything at the beginning, but if you have to go back months later, there's the possibility that you wouldn't be able to accurately recall the information anymore.

That's why it's a smart move to organize your information from the beginning. If this is not done from the start, it can become a chaotic mess as you start to expand.

There's a saying that it only takes ninety seconds to make a great impression when you meet someone for the first time. You need to go in prepared, having practiced everything you're going to do or say. Don't land a pitch meeting only to stammer or stumble on your words.

To avoid a scenario like this, the first and most important thing is, as we mentioned earlier, knowing your story and being ready to share it. No retailer wants to hear about your personal life for ten or thirty minutes.

Why?

Because the pitch is not about you. It's about them. You're going to make them money. Sum it up like an elevator speech. Talk about who you are, what your company represents, what your brand is, your mission and vision, and what you can do for them, and you will see results.

If you're unsure about what an elevator speech is, just imagine yourself going in an elevator, floor-to-floor, maybe one to two minutes max, and in walks the one person who has the ability to help make your dreams come true. If only you can convince them before they reach their stop…

You will have share all the important information in a quick, well-organized manner to make that lasting impression before your target reaches their destination. That's all the time you get.

Your pitch needs to express a lot in a very short time, so proper development is key. Your content needs to be very rich and empowering while delivering a clear message.

You also need to back up your claims with statistics. If you're a new product or brand, that's a risk for them.

Statistics inspire confidence from potential buyers in several ways.

- Back the viability of your product.
- Indicate how big the industry is and how much money is being made.
- Show you are solving a problem within that industry and how.

The retailer wants you to prove that their customers will want to buy your product and that the retailer will make money. Your stats are proof.

Where can you get these statistics? You might throw in some numbers that indicate how often people purchase your product. For example, if you sell on Amazon, you could give Amazon sales statistics. How many sales do you make in a day?

They want to know where they're coming from, how many are they reordering, and who your competitors are. All this can be summarized because your pitch is, in a sense, a summary. You have to throw in the hard facts and details that are going to impress them so that they see your product as an opportunity. That's what the pitch is —showing the retailer that you present a huge opportunity for their customers, and for them to make money.

Remember, the whole pitch should be no more than five to ten minutes long. We've seen pitches of fifteen or twenty minutes, but this usually happens when the retailer dictates the length. You also need to have an even shorter version ready for when you unexpectedly meet someone at a trade show. For this type of quick introduction, you need to have a sixty-second elevator pitch.

They'll also have questions.

- What does your product do that's different from other similar products that are out there?
- Why are you here telling us this?

You need to be ready with the answers.

You need to make them feel confident that your product will help their customers. You can respond by saying, for example, "We're here to help your customers," "We're supporting your customers," or, "We have a product for your loyal customers." This approach will ensure that they think, "Wow, this person is genuinely interested in helping my company grow in this product line to service my customers."

Everything doesn't always go according to plan. You might think you have given the best pitch ever and still get a "no." Sometimes, it is straightforward and you get a "yes." Other times, it's a "no" for obvious reasons. Sometimes the response you get is simply out of your control, but if you walk in unprepared, only talking about you and unable to answer their questions, then the meeting won't be pretty.

Make sure your pitch is an extension of you. If you're a happy person with a product that will help people, solving problems and making lives easier, then your pitch should reflect positivity. Retailers want to deal with someone who will be easy to work with. You should walk in clear on your vision, clear on your mission, clear on your product. It will make things a lot simpler for the person who's going to make the decision to accept your product or not.

We'd like to add that it's not enough to just know your story. Yes, you know where you came from, how you developed, and how you got into your current position, but if you're unable to correctly articulate that, then the right information won't be conveyed. If you don't effectively articulate, your words can have unintended meanings. Poorly spoken words can cause embarrassment and potentially affect the retailer's final decision.

Most of the time, when people buy a product, they buy it based on emotional sentiments. The same can be said for pitching your brand and product: It's a psychological journey. When you give your speech, you build recognition and credibility, and begin to appeal to the retailer's emotions. Your audience—the retailers—are, in every sense, buying your brand. They make purchases to stock your products in their stores, so the emotion you share must resonate with them as well.

The story, mission, and vision of your brand should be crafted to influence emotion. When we talked about personalizing the pitch, such as including names of prior contacts, the point was to begin building an emotional element, by triggering a sense of trust and a desire to hear more of what you have to say. If you do this, the human connection will shine through—because, at the end of the day, helping other humans is what you do.

We work with several coaches, service providers, small businesses, and entrepreneurs who have been on a journey during the course of their story. They all have a vision, a mission to help. They care and are motivated to make positive changes in people's lives. That shows not only when they're speaking, but also in their business. It's reflected in their products.

You must include this in your narrative because you want retailers to understand what your business means to you. That's why salespeople are still crucial to businesses today. Even with the high functionality of computers, we still need people to convey the story and make that human connection. This is what creates the connections that lead to customer loyalty.

WHO ARE YOU PITCHING TO?

There are several types of people you could pitch to, including retail store owners, assistant buyers, and buying teams. Each type is different and requires a unique approach, so it's important to know who you'll meet to tailor your pitch. Ultimately, this factor dictates the length of the process.

Sometimes, the whole process can take months. It could take up to a year, during which you don't know if you're making headway. You don't know who's reading the emails or who's getting the information you plan to present. If you communicate directly with the owner of the company, and they're involved in the decision-making process, it's most likely that the process will be short. We consider this the best approach and always advise our clients to go after the owner.

This is not always possible when working with big chains like Target, Walmart, and Bed, Bath, and Beyond. These chains have buying groups—department buyers, category buyers, regional buyers, and even a national buyer. They break it down because they see thousands of products every day.

This needs to be understood. If you have something that fits into a generic category, such as soaps, they have hundreds and hundreds of soaps on their shelves. The question then becomes, "What's going to distinguish your brand and make your product different?"

In the larger retail stores, the chain typically starts with a buyer and an assistant. Usually, the buyer filters everything through the assistant who looks at all the products and decides if they're a good fit for their proposed category.

The type of buyer is also categorized. If you walk into Walmart, for example, you'll find different sections such as the beauty section, the kid's section, the maternity section, the toy section, and the electronics section. For each section, there's a buyer. You may have been talking to the buyer for the camping section, but your product's appropriate category is pets.

To avoid a scenario like that, make sure that you are connected to the right people so you can pitch to the right person. The last thing you want is to expend your energy pitching to the one person who's not going to make any decision at all. They'll only say, "No, it's not for us."

You'll wonder if it's time to send all your hard work to the Product Graveyard, when you're just in front of the wrong person.

Remember that not all buyers are created equal. Some buyers don't even have decision-making rights. You might make your pitch to a buyer who will say, "Okay. I'll take the information and pass it on," even though they can't.

Sometimes, it's not just a direct "meet with the buyer and get a yes or no answer" sequence of events. Sometimes you'll get the right person the first time, and they will give you a yes or no.

In many cases, there's a next level, then a next level—like peeling layer after layer of an onion until you get to the real decision-makers.

It all comes back to building your channels of communication and keeping them open. Don't take anything personally as you navigate the various levels of buyers' groups. When you have a connection with someone, your goal should be to build upon that relationship.

WHAT HAPPENS AFTER THE PITCH?

After you conclude your pitch, your potential client may say, "Great, we'll get back to you and let you know what our final decision is."

Usually, this feedback will come in the form of an email, letter, or phone call. Sometimes, they'll tell you right then and there if it's a "yes" or a "no." More often than not, you will hear a "no."

As a business owner, you are passionate about your business; your brand, vision, and mission; and your products. Because you are so married to your business, it's easy to take criticism personally. And yes, "no" hurts! Don't take it personally though, because, as we mentioned earlier, "no" doesn't always mean "no" forever.

If you have a high-quality product that is backed up by its history, reviews documenting how it's changing lives, high sales, and other positives, then it's likely that the product is not the issue when you get a negative response.

A rejection might mean:

- The product is not a right fit for the store at that moment.
- The buyer was just having a really bad day.
- The buyer is new to this category and inexperienced.

You never know what's going on in people's lives, and personal events can be a factor. Once again, don't take any rejection personally. Just keep moving forward. If you have a top-quality product, a "yes" will soon follow.

Feedback will help you moving forward. Use the information and feedback that comes with rejections to make needed modifications. Record all of the information you've gathered from the places that rejected you. You should revisit them later for follow-ups.

You can also ask after the pitch,

- "Can you tell me what exactly I need to work on?"
- "Why do you feel my brand is not a good fit for you and potentially other buyers?"

If you ask these questions, some buyers will oblige you and offer helpful responses. Some companies have specific guidelines for anything from packaging to messaging. Perhaps they didn't understand that you're flexible and willing to change it.

Their response to your questions will give you insight into what you need to do better next time. We'll explore the psychology of rejection more comprehensively in the next chapter.

We're often asked if giving samples is a good idea. Buyers love samples, but whether or not providing them is a good idea is an ongoing discussion that we have all the time.

The answer is that it depends on the cost of the samples, how many you have readily available to you, and who they're going to. If you're pitching new microwaves and they're expensive, you wouldn't necessarily leave samples.

Via email, you may get a lot of generic responses that say, "Thank you so much for your inquiry. Please send us a sample." When pitching via email, you can decide if it's worth it for you or not. If you decide to send a sample, be sure to follow up and track the sample, ensuring that it is seen by someone who matters.

At a face-to-face meeting, you need to bring a sample along to show what the product looks like. We recommend that you bring a sample that you can leave behind as well. Because they have taken the time to give you a face-to-face audience and listen to your pitch, bringing a sample is a must.

Often the buyer will say, "Just leave us a sample, and we'll get back to you." If you only have three samples ready, you might be giving out one to buyers who are not that intrigued about your product.

Let's say you've created a new type of sports equipment for the hockey industry and the store you're meeting is a place for hockey enthusiasts. When he says, "Sure, leave us a sample," he might not have any intention of adding it to his store, but instead wants the sample for himself.

To forestall this, go in prepared to read the people you're meeting with. Watch them closely and see how they react to the product before deciding whether to leave a sample or not.

After the meeting, revisit and analyze the situation, their reaction, and how serious they were. If they talked about placing an order, of course you'd want to leave a sample or arrange to have one sent.

Sometimes, you don't need to send the sample—or even talk about it—because you can show what the product looks like in a short video presentation. Take those emails and the responses you get in return and turn them into live meetings.

If you receive, "Yes, send us a sample," in response to a

first query email, encourage them to invite you for a face-to-face meeting. Reply that you would love to give them a sample, and it would be a thrill to deliver it in person.

Some time ago, we tried to get into a major and well-known retail store in New York. Although we sold to other retailers in the market at the time, this one retailer had a store in our prime location. We knew our products would fit them perfectly, but getting a meeting was impossible. Because we were local, we called the store.

The woman who answered the phone happened to be the owner's wife, and she was only taking calls because the assistant had called in sick that day.

We knew who the owners were—we did our research—and instantly recognized her last name. We told her we were in New York, how much we loved their store, and that we were at a competitor's store filling out a display of our product which was selling very well in the city. We offered to stop by their store and show her the product.

By the end of the conversation, we left her no doubt that the product would be a wonderful fit for their fantastic store and customers.

Right away, she put us through to her husband. It was a golden chance and we were prepared; that was how we knew the store owners' names in the first place. We improvised and had a bit of luck, but if we hadn't done our homework and been prepared and ready to pitch, the opportunity would have slipped out of our grasp.

When you're making these connections, you have to act

like a detective, uncovering information about different people and stores, and deducing how your product fits in it with them.

You also have to take on the role of salesperson and human connector because you need to continually nourish those relationships.

This is one reason why we have so much respect for product creators and product developers who get their products into the stores. Not only do they tackle the difficult development work, they also need the stamina and endurance to push their product to retailers.

You have to do your homework, think quickly on your feet, and be in for the long haul. If it was easy, everybody would do it.

For many years after our meeting that day, the owner of that store in New York made it a point to send one of their buyers to our booth whenever we were at a trade show. During the year, they'd have their new buyers call us—even if we hadn't received an order in months—to ask if we had anything new.

This was only possible because of that first impression we created years ago. It made the difference, giving us access to their store for years to come because they knew that we would always share quality products.

Success stories are wonderful. They can provide necessary encouragement to stick it out. But don't lose track of this fact: the majority of pitches will result in a "no." This is inevitable.

For a retail store, taking on a new product is a risk. If most products were accepted, the shelves wouldn't be able to hold all of the new products.

Kathryn Goetzke designed Mood-lites, colorful interior lights that she felt were destined for success if she could only penetrate the interior lighting market. To cut through the noise, she decided she needed to convince retailers that her product would dovetail with a consumer trend.

The inspiration came when she saw an advertisement for Home Depot that used color therapy to sell wall paint. She developed this idea, working her psychology background to reframe her product around the concept of color therapy.

With the help of her husband, she created several public relations articles in magazines to both sell Mood-Lites and also sell their story to potential retailers.

She was able to use these articles as part of her pitch when approaching retailers. She pursued massage therapists, yoga instructors, and other professionals concerned with establishing a relaxing environment to make her first sales and build word of mouth. Goetzke was able to approach her pitch meetings with the momentum of a trend behind her—one she helped create.

This just goes to show that there is no limit to the creativity you can levy when selling your product. Indeed, the ingenuity you apply in your approach to your pitch meetings might equal that in the development of your product!

———

TIPS

1. PREPARE YOUR PITCH! Have it ready. You never know when an opportunity might come along.
2. REMEMBER: your goal is to get in front of the decision-makers.
3. START WITH QUERY EMAILS, TRADE SHOWS, OR OTHER IN-PERSON POSSIBILITIES. Even virtual meetings are fantastic. Be open to that first step!
4. HAVE PRODUCT SAMPLES READY. But distribute them wisely.

Remember, it's all about building relationships. At the end of the day, it all starts with showing that you have something good to offer through your pitch. Other circumstances, like luck or good timing, might come into play, but from the moment you make that first impression, you begin to build the relationship.

You must be as meticulously prepared as possible in order to take advantage of these opportunities. Once your foot is in the door, the process becomes much easier, but the pitch is your first—and sometimes only—chance to keep that door from slamming shut in your face. If you're ready with a passionate and well-prepared pitch the door might swing open and invite you in.

ARE YOU TRULY RETAIL READY?

Individuals frequently ask us, "Will my brand be on the retail shelves?" That is the million-dollar question. We wish we had a crystal ball and could give a concrete answer, but that is impossible. What we can say is that you have a phenomenal chance of getting on shelves if you are truly retail-ready.

Is it safe to say your products are Retail Ready? Let's have a look... Have you done the following:

CHECKLIST

1. HAVE YOU DONE YOUR RESEARCH? Do your schoolwork! Visit and understand the stores you need to be in (or if nothing else, look at their website) and see what makes that retailer the right place for your product and brand before reaching out to buyer.
2. IS YOUR PRESENTATION RETAIL READY? Is your packaging correct for the type of retailer you are pitching to? Do you have the right legal information and testing done for that market?
3. DO YOU HAVE A STORY AND VISION BEHIND YOUR BRAND? Buyers need to associate with the individual or business behind the brand and hear your story.
4. ARE YOUR WEBSITE AND SOCIAL MEDIA PLATFORMS

PROFESSIONAL? The first thing a buyer will do is Google your website and check out what people are saying about your brand. Make sure your online collateral expresses your brand and highlights your products. Your essence on the web will show the buyer that you pay attention to your business. It's also a great way for buyers to see what you can offer before meeting with you.

5. DO YOU HAVE A LINE SHEET OR SALES SHEET? Buyers are constantly inundated with product entries. Stand out from the group by having a line sheet that includes all the crucial information that buyers need to compose a buy request: costs and pricing, SRP, SKUs, barcodes, discounts, terms and conditions, shipping, and MOQ.

6. DO YOU KNOW YOUR COMPETITION? Determine who your competitors are, so you can speak confidently about what makes your line different, and how it fills a void in the market. You can throw in stats and numbers that impress.

7. DO YOU HAVE A POWERFUL PITCH REHEARSED AND READY? You can't wing it, not with so much riding on your successful pitch.

8. DO YOU HAVE SAMPLES? If you are meeting face to face samples are mandatory.

9. HAVE YOU CONSIDERED MARKETING? Stores need to know that you are doing your part in getting the word out about your brand. Past sales, reviews, and

testimonials are so important to share with the buyer. They want to know you will support them in getting traffic into their stores, so share your plan.

10. ARE YOU CONFIDENT? You must walk in with your head high and share your love of your brand and product. Help the buyers to fall in love, too.

CHAPTER 4
HOW TO DEAL WITH "NO"

Our focus in this chapter is on the psychology of rejection. It's a fact of life. How do you deal with it? Nobody likes to hear the word "no," but it is the go-to word in this industry. How can we best prepare for it?

The word "no" appeared several times in the previous chapter. If you're serious about building your retail business, you will experience a lot of rejection. It's unfortunate but inevitable.

Success is the result of careful planning, the right attitude, and the ability to maturely deal with setbacks. If you're crushed by every rejection, you'll never prevail in your goals. Inability to properly process a "no" can interfere with your journey, vision, and direction. Rejections can happen for any reason, and often have nothing to do with you at all.

This makes the ability to navigate your rejection even more

important; otherwise, you're letting external factors undermine your worth and derail your approach. At the same time, rejections can also be part of a learning curve. They provide lessons that you can use to improve your next pitching experience.

People who take steps to prepare themselves for rejection increase their chances of succeeding compared to someone who is taken completely off guard by a negative response. Although this preparation takes effort and energy, when faced with subsequent rejections, you'll be extremely confident about your ability to deal with it and better prepared to learn from the experience so you can move on.

An important concept underpinning our discussion of rejections is the simple fact that it's much easier to say "no" than it is to say "yes." You're asking people to take a chance on an unknown quantity, on an unknown product and idea, to risk their resources on you and your product. They might hear any number of pitches regularly in the course of their business and can only afford to consider very few of them.

Logically and statistically, "no" is the answer that is going to make sense in the vast majority of exchanges. No matter how perfectly you pitch your product, there's a very small chance that yours will be that perfect fit, the pitch that rises to the top above all of the others.

This is not to incite despair; it's just a reflection of reality. You're going to hear "no." It's part of the game, not a negative reflection on your plan or your product. You must be prepared for it.

Don't let rejections, which truly are par for the course, undermine your confidence. To the contrary, if you know the value of your project and your vision, you shouldn't let a "no" sway you at all. It's just an indicator that you're putting your product out there and can be seen as a step towards your eventual success.

We had a client who shared a story of how his father would always answer "no" to every request. It didn't matter what you asked, whether it was an important or trivial matter, the automatic response was always a negative.

After years of witnessing this, the client realized that "no" didn't always really mean "no." Often, it meant "not now." Once he'd learned to translate his father's responses, he went in prepared. When he was about to ask his dad for something, he'd prepare himself for the inevitable "no" because he knew there was a chance of eventually turning the initial negative response to a "yes."

His experience with his father while growing up prepared him for his later life and business dealings. On certain occasions, he'd go in to pitch a product and get rejected. Instead of feeling sad about it, he'd simply brush it off as wrong timing. A "no" can be a crack in the door that you can eventually widen into a "yes." It can be an indication that, with the right timing, the negative can be turned into a positive. It need not be viewed pessimistically at all.

Another client was asked to come and make a pitch for his product to a well-known retailer. He showed up on the day of the appointment and nervously waited to be called in. Soon, it was time, and he walked into the owner's office. Inside was a large boardroom table. At the far end sat the owner, who looked like he couldn't have been much more than five feet tall.

Our client began his pitch. The owner listened patiently, even though he knew exactly why our client was there. After his detailed explanation about the product line and how it would be a no-brainer product for the retailer because they didn't have anything like it, the owner said, "We're not interested."

Our client was taken aback by the response. The retailer had called for the meeting and asked him to fly all the way from Canada to New York.

For what? He wondered.

Apparently, just to say, "Thank you, but I'm not interested." It was something he could have easily been told him over the phone.

Instead of leaving, our client decided to wait outside. It was still morning, which meant he had the whole day to wait. A lady came around and asked him what he was waiting for. He told her he'd forgotten to explain something clearly to the owner.

She said, "Well, he's got a very busy schedule."

"That's okay," he said. "I don't mind waiting."

Eventually, the owner stepped out of the office.

"What are you doing here?" he asked. "Didn't you hear what I said?"

"I did," our client replied. "But you know what? There was

something I forgot to mention. I know it would be good for your other stores, possibly in Florida and Georgia. Just let me show you this information..."

The owner said "no" again, but this time allowed our client to leave his catalog and samples. This was an important step because these would serve as something the owner could reference, and as a reminder of our client and his product.

Over the next twelve months, our client persisted with the owner. He found out the reason for his initial rejection much later. The owner had a habit of demonstrating his authority whenever he met someone for the first time. Saying "no" was his way of achieving this. He did it to everybody. It was nothing personal.

However, our client was convinced that his product was a good fit and persisted until he got the chance for another meeting. After meeting with the owner again, he was approved and soon had his product in twenty of their locations. Through the process, he was confident that they would ultimately see the value in the brand. He simply needed to go through their circuits.

In a similar scenario, many people would take the rejection personally. They'd let it lead them to question whether or not they had the right product. They would turn back, go home, and miss the opportunity because they weren't prepared enough to realize that, in the world of business, "no" doesn't necessarily mean "no."

Anything can go on behind the scenes. The person you see might be having a bad day. They could be in the middle of a personal deliberation to leave the company. Perhaps their expenses are done for that quarter when happened to come by. They might tell you, "We can't buy any more right now," but don't come out and say, "Come back next month." They want to leave it up to you to see if you will be persistent.

Although this might seem like a mind game, it's also a way for them to learn something about you. If you're persistent, it implies you're serious about your business. You're a hard worker. If you don't take that initial "no" for an answer, you establish yourself as a force to be reckoned with. Owners like to see confidence. Nothing is less appealing than a seller who's not sure of himself. If you're not even confident in yourself, why should anyone sign on with you?

The initial "no" can be viewed as serving a gatekeeping function. They're testing you. They want to know if you can deliver. If you show that you are invested and persistent, they'll be more likely to take in your product. That first rejection doesn't mean there won't be other opportunities to get a positive answer.

If you know how to handle rejection well, you can turn it into a future opportunity. Accept their answer, but tell them, "Great, maybe this is something you might want to consider in the future. Let me leave you some samples and check back in a few months."

Instead of taking it personally and walking away, be persistent. A "no" can be an opportunity to "play the long game." Even as you're on your way out the door after receiving your rejection, you can plant seeds that will eventually sprout into an affirmative answer.

The hardest part of getting rejected can be the uncertainty it brings. Most people desperately want to know the reason for the rejection, yet many will be too scared to ask why. As a default, they consider themselves lesser than those they're pitching to.

If you make a pitch, it's important to consider it a conversation between equals. To be successful, you must have the mindset that you're there to help them as much as they are there to help you.

It's true, isn't it?

If you truly believe in your pitch, your product, and yourself, then you must believe that you have something to offer. Don't undercut yourself by exuding desperation. It's no more attractive to a potential buyer than it is to a potential romantic partner. Confidence and belief in what you're selling will set their minds at ease.

It doesn't matter the size of the store or market. All stores, no matter their size or who their owner is, are equal. They're all potential clients that you need to have a conversation with to get what you want and give them what they need, even if they don't realize they need it yet.

Whether they are celebrities or big retailers, ultimately they're people just like you. They have families waiting for them at home and do the same things that you do. Even if they're millionaires, they have mouths to feed, bills to pay, kids to put through college. It's only a matter of scale. The only real difference is they have more money because they've developed their business already. Apart from that, they're just like you.

Go in with the mindset that you're talking to equals. Remind yourself of this if you need to. Take a minute; stand in front of the mirror before the big pitch and remind yourself that you're no different than the people you're pitching to.

Don't psych yourself out and treat the person sitting across the table as if they're better or more worthy than you. Then you're likely to grow fearful, or too deferential and apologetic. If you go in with a negative mindset, it'll inevitably feed into your pitch. They'll see your doubt in yourself and assume that you also feel that way about your product.

Regardless of whether you go in with the correct frame of mind, it's no assurance of accomplishment. As we've stated, there are extraordinary quantities of reasons that you may be turned down. A considerable number of them have nothing to do with you or the innate estimation of your product or nature of your pitch. If you have a product of extraordinary worth, that you realize will be a solid match for a retailer's store, and they disapprove of it after your pitch, it's imperative not to overthink it.

It's not about you. It's important to remember it is their business and their decision in the end. Keeping your options open and finding another home for your product is the next step and the next opportunity.

If you've been rejected, then it's up to you to take away something valuable from it. Your next step should be to learn from the rejection and get back to the drawing board to develop another strategy.

Remember when we said that many don't even bother asking for feedback because they feel scared or unworthy? Don't make that mistake.

If you've been rejected but before that door closes behind you, it is incumbent upon you to ask for feedback, politely and without a hint of resentment or bitterness. You should want the feedback because it will be useful. It might be crucial in developing your pitch to the point that it will move your product from your garage onto retail shelves.

The information contained in post-pitch feedback can help you identify that secret missing ingredient. With this new knowledge you can be better prepared when you re-approach the same retailer or meet with others.

For the record, you should do both. Never limit yourself to one retailer. There are so many out there. Even if you have in your head that one particular retailer will favor you, leave your options open. You might be surprised.

Learn what there is to learn and then move on. Get back to work. Staying in one place and mulling over a rejection takes more energy than getting your nose back to the grindstone and turning a "no" to a "yes."

Getting comfortable with rejection and understanding what it means may take a little counter-programming. Many people live their lives in fear of rejection or failure. They don't take risks because they're afraid of hearing a "no." These people will never succeed because they'll never put themselves out on a limb.

Those who go places take those first steps, even when they can't say for sure what the immediate outcome will be. Rejection, in itself, gives you critical feedback that you can then apply to get yourself where you need to go. Take the accumulated rejections as pieces of a puzzle. When you get a no, see it as a missing piece that you can fit into the big picture.

Rejection creates an energy that can either turn into something positive or negative. Negative energy will consume you and guarantee further failure. If you choose the victim mindset, the energy will only hold you down.

With a positive mindset the same energy can be channeled toward your success. It can impel you to ask questions like, "What can I learn?" and "How can I grow?" You could tap into positive rejection energy and use it as an opportunity to reevaluate your sales approach and assess the strength of your pitch.

It's understandable that you sometimes get wrapped up and personally invested in your products. It's easy enough to say, "don't take it personally," but when you've poured hours and money and blood, sweat, and tears into your operation, it's easier said than done. It's hard to personally take a bird's eye view of a business situation when you've poured your heart and soul into it.

That's why you need to work with a coach or some other neutral outsider who can help you evaluate your product objectively. This outsider's perspective will help you shape what your pitch will be like, whom you're going to pitch to, and will make sure you truly are retail ready. When you work with a coach who can see things from a different angle, it will make a world of difference to your approach towards rejection and help you to better understand it.

Second opinions are crucial. When you're the only voice and the only perspective, you can miss important things. For this same reason, moves are shown to test audiences and people go to therapists with their personal issues. You can only get so far when locked in your head and your limited perspective.

One piece of advice we often give people is to stay connected to their retailers, even when they've been rejected. We've discussed the role of social media in previous chapters, this also comes into play here. You can stay in touch with retailers via social media platforms such as Facebook, Instagram, and LinkedIn to see what's happening on their end. Even when you're not in direct contact, it's important to keep track of retailer you might eventually revisit.

Many things can change on their end. Buyers might go work with another company and, despite telling you no initially, have your product and ideas in mind. If you remain connected, those buyers might be open to bringing your product to their new company because the circumstances have changed.

Because of the ever-changing nature of the business world, it's always important to leave on a positive note, even when you have to initially take no for an answer. Never leave on a negative, as you don't know what the future holds. If you burn bridges then you won't have the chance to re-pitch when conditions might favor you.

Feedback can go further than just refining a pitch. If your company can easily change a product, the ideas garnered in a feedback session after a rejected pitch can be used to improve your product as well.

Some time ago, we designed some products with Barnes and Noble in mind. We took it to a trade show, and the representatives of Barnes and Noble came by to take a look. We could see they had a lot of interest in it but ultimately decided not to take it. Just as they were about to leave, we asked them, "Did you like the product?"

They told us that they loved it, but wished it had other features. We took note of their comments, and they asked if we had any products with the features they'd mentioned. We told them no, thanked them for their feedback, and exchanged business cards.

We could have made the changes they suggested the next day, but instead, we spent the next month making up new samples, incorporating all the information they'd given to us. Their response to the updates was positive; they loved the product and ended up making an order for it.

We had stayed connected to them since we already knew what they were looking for. Although we didn't have the kind of product they wanted at the time they asked, we knew we could make changes and were able to eventually get the product into their stores.

There's a feedback and testing loop, just like there is with any market. You have to listen to the feedback, evaluate it, determine if you can make changes, then endeavor to deliver exactly what the market wants.

We encourage you to not disregard external feedback. You probably think you already have the perfect product, and maybe you do. But feedback should always be welcomed as new ideas can open up more opportunties.

This underscores why it's so important to have a coach. It's not compulsory to have one, but if you want the process to be smooth and fast, some sort of outside support is advantageous.

One of the things our clients love about us is that we have a unique perspective on the process of retail. Because we have been in the physical product industry for over 3 decades, we have been blessed with the knowledge and expertise of being on both sides of retail. We have been:

1. a retail brick-and-mortar owner where brand owners pitch to us, and
2. a product owner pitching to other retailers.

This aids us greatly in our understanding of the big picture because we play both sides. We understand what's happening from all angles and, as a result, can make sure our clients are truly retail-ready and will have success. Having been on both sides, we have been able to dissect the pitching and buying process to aid in success on both sides.

WHAT IS THE MEANING OF A NO IF YOU ARE RETAIL-READY AND YOU PRESENTED AN AWESOME PITCH?

Most often, the "no" comes from something that can't be delivered. That's why it's so important to prepare and practice for every conceivable contingency. We have a story of someone we worked with who pitched to a retailer. The presentation was well-received, but the buyer didn't make an order. After some digging, we were able to determine why they didn't follow through. The product owner didn't have the capacity to fulfill the order. This is one of the biggest reasons retail stores lose interest.

Let's say the retailer wanted ten thousand units of the product, or maybe they wanted them in six thousand stores. In any case, the production rate did not look like it could be meet the needs quickly enough, so the retailer ultimately declined.

In a case like this, it's a mistake to consider it a true "no." This type of rejection sends the message that you need to clean up your act, get your production rate up to speed, and go back in there prepared. The worst thing you could do under these circumstances is give up and miss out on the potential for follow-up opportunities.

Another reason for rejection is a lack of belief. Do you actually believe in yourself? Ask yourself if you really believe your product is the best option for customers. You must also determine if you believe that you are the best person to introduce the product to the market. If you have any doubt in yourself, your confidence in the product won't show through.

To achieve belief, you have to be married to your product. You need to live, eat, sleep, breathe, and dream your product. Sometimes, you won't be able to do this alone. Surround yourself with people who can see beyond the things that you're seeing. Let their perceptions and advice buoy your energy.

When someone starts a conversation with you about something they don't have much information about, or a passion or desire for, you probably zone out and offer only polite responses. If the same person comes to you with passion, desire, knowledge, concern, empathy, and reasons why what they're talking about could change your life, then you listen. Emotion can have a big influence on decision-making, particularly when it is sincere.

We often advise people that it is better to be rejected than ignored. This way, you know where you stand and what your next step should be. Getting an outright rejection also confirms this: Someone listened. It's better to get a definite "No, it doesn't fit in our store," response than to never risk rejection. A response like this allows you to know where you stand and decide on your next move.

When you're a pro at handling rejection, then you're ready to tackle anything this business throws at you.

CHAPTER 5
RETAIL PHD

You've made it this far: The retailers have accepted your product. They love it. Retailers are now ready to take your product to the next level.

The question is: are you ready?

This chapter will present you with a checklist of everything you need to consider, plan, and then complete as you make your first sales in retail stores a reality. This is the point where some heavy-duty logistics come in.

Up to this point, you may have been working on a smaller scale and at your own pace. Now, you're in the big leagues and have deadlines and order requirements to meet.

This chapter will give you everything you need: the keys to success when working with retail and chain stores and a clear understanding of what you should expect. Once you've put these tools into practice and successfully fulfilled that first order, consider yourself granted your Retail Ready doctorate.

As we've emphasized before, your psychology is important. It's crucial you avoid being nervous. You already know your product and should be confident in it. There is no need to feel intimidated because you've already gotten through the door. They've signed off on your product. Rejection and fears are no longer relevant.

At this point you should also be armed with knowledge about your mission. You're working with people who potentially love your product as well.

Now you have a lot of work ahead of you. There will be many things to do—many plates to keep spinning. You need to stay on top of it. There is no room for procrastination; do what you need to do as you need to do it.

THE PURCHASE ORDER

The first item on our checklist is a purchase order establishing the agreement between you and the buyer. This is a very important step and nothing should proceed without it.

All orders are created equal, because all stores, no matter how big or small, want superb products on their shelves.

Remember, though, that even if you're working with a very small retailer, everything needs to be done professionally. By doing this, you establish yourself as a businessperson and protect yourself by formalizing expectations.

When someone says, "Hey, we're doing business. I'd like to

order fifty units," they have not yet truly made an order. It's great news that they want your product, but a verbal statement isn't enough.

If the retailer changes his or her mind, there is no contractual obligation. He might have forgotten what you discussed in the past. A week later, you might swear he said fifty and he might remember a different figure.

Before proceeding, you need to record your purchase order. Everything has to be written, typed, and emailed to all relevant parties. A concrete paper trail is necessary to establish that the retailer is placing an order.

In the good old days, a handshake may have sufficed, but the world has changed. Now you need guarantees. If you are preparing for an order of 50,000 units, you need more than a handshake to ensure that you're not left sitting on that inventory after the retailer has second thoughts.

Even if your buyer doesn't think it's necessary, insist on a purchase order. It will protect both parties from misunderstanding and potential disagreement.

While no order should proceed without a purchase order, there is another piece of paperwork that should also be established, providing a broader umbrella of established understanding between you and the retailer: the contract.

THE CONTRACT

Anytime you do business with a large retailer, there will be a contract to go along with a purchase order. They will also give you a booklet of the rules, regulations, conditions, and terms for how they do business.

This is a guideline to show you what they require—a binding booklet that helps you fully understand the requirements of the business relationship that you're entering.

Typically, large chains such as Home Depot, Michaels, Hobby Lobby, and Walmart have these documents. Some smaller chain stores may not, preferring to rely on the rapport and trust they have established with sellers.

The contractual relationship with the larger retailers may start with you filling out a vendor agreement with their company to get a vendor number.

The vendor agreement acts as the contract in many cases, but the contract doesn't always have to come from the retailer. You, too, can present a retailer with a contract of your own with terms and conditions.

Most retail contracts lay out the terms of agreement and outline the relationship of the retailer and the vendor.

For instance, if you're supplying the retailer with art material for their stores, the contract may specify certain health and safety documents and testing data to be disclosed prior to selling in that retailer. These are required in addition to all the basic and rudimentary terms and conditions like shipping details, insurance, payment terms, late fees, and quotas.

———

TIPS

1. HAVE AN ATTORNEY REVIEW YOUR CONTRACT, REGARDLESS OF HOW STRAIGHTFORWARD IT LOOKS. The contract is an important item on the checklist and should not be entered into lightly. Remember, this is a legally binding document. You're establishing obligations on your part that may have legal implications. Before signing, it is important that you have a full understanding of what is being contractually required from you to them and vice versa. Make sure a lawyer is involved for more clarification.

2. YOU SHOULD LIKEWISE HAVE THE CONTRACT AUTHORIZED. It is a rookie mistake to proceed with a contract you don't completely comprehend or didn't even read. Protect yourself from surprises, just as the retailer naturally will.

When both parties understand expectations, it's easier for them to trust each other and treat each other as equals. It removes guesswork from the equation and allows for better communication and a more smoothly functioning business relationship—a relationship dictated by the specific deal formalized in the contract.

As we've established, some smaller retailers may be ready to proceed without a contract. Although there is the chance you might be able to have a positive experience without one, you shouldn't take that chance. It is advisable not to deal with any retailer without signing a legal contract with them. You're setting yourself up for a potentially negative experience because you're leaving the basic terms of your relationship nebulous.

If you work with a smaller retailer that doesn't prepare a contract, take the opportunity to work with a lawyer to develop one on your own.

If your retailer is serious about working with you, they'll indulge you on the paperwork. And it's practical; it will help them understand your terms and conditions. After the contract has been signed you can proceed with the purchase order coming from that retailer.

At trade shows, buyers will walk around with a purchase order sheet so that they can make orders of products they love on the spot. You may have to wait for their terms and conditions, which they'll send to clarify, for example, whether your products should ship to one warehouse location or to individual stores.

With the larger chains, the contract will immediately follow the PO because they may want to order it right at the show. If you're at a trade show and only receive a purchase order, ask if they have a vendor agreement or contract. Generally speaking, they'll send you one in short order.

Once you get your purchase order, it's important to carefully review it. Not all purchase orders are the same. The layout may be different from what you're accustomed to, making it difficult to find what you're looking for. Check for small boxes that indicate where it's being shipped to and other important information. Make sure all the information is correct.

The price you quoted them should be the same as the one that appears on the purchase order. Companies make mistakes, and double-checking your agreement is in your own best interests.

Billing information and where you will ship to are of primary concern. Many companies will place your billing to one corporate office while you ship it to different district warehouses. For this reason, you should crosscheck every detail of the order thoroughly. Don't assume that the first address you see on the order is your shipping destination.

Companies make shipping decisions for a variety of reasons. One of these is a rollout. The company may want the products shipped to many different addresses as new products in October after ordering in January. Make sure you're both on the same page.

Naturally, you're excited at this point. You can't wait to ship that order as soon as you get back from the trade show.

Communication is very vital at every stage of the journey. Make sure you maintain open channels of communication with designated representatives of the company. Clarify any open questions and confirm with them the date of shipping and address.

Big companies have numerous shipments arriving every day, and it's important that you meet their terms and that your order arrives with a packing list to guarantee that the order is properly input. The packing list will show that the product comes from your company and goes to the warehouse indicated, as well as the items and quantity in the shipment.

A packing list has similar details to the purchase order with the exception of pricing. Sometimes an order will require two or three packing lists if orders are going to different parts of the warehouse.

Make sure this is its own document. Don't include your invoice as those contain a lot of confidential information. A packing list arrives before the invoice and in the order itself when shipping.

The invoice, which includes the pricing and payment amount, is only sent to the company's billing contact who will pay for the order.

Filling out the checklists properly is vital to avoid a scenario where your product is incorrectly placed. In an unfortunate example of this, one of our clients who deals in medical supplies got their package misrouted because it was categorized as meat. The shipment of medical supplies was placed in the frozen section at the retailer. If your shipment is properly labeled, you will avoid this kind of situation.

Another important consideration: some packages need special documentation. For instance, if you're shipping food products, cosmetic products, spray paints, or certain adhesives, you will need to include a hazmat certification.

You should also enclose safety data sheets, because without them the trucking company may not be able to deliver your shipment to its intended destination.

NEIL AND KAREN GWARTZMAN

Once your products have reached their destination and the company has confirmed receipt, you can relax.

Congratulations, you've earned it. For your benefit, however, here are some tips on what to avoid once you've shipped that first order:

TIPS

1. DON'T CALL THEM THE DAY AFTER YOU'VE SHIPPED AND SAY, "HEY, I HAVE MORE PRODUCTS I WANT TO PITCH TO YOU." Once they get your product, they want to begin selling and see if they are generating profit. Do not be that pushy salesperson.

2. DON'T TELL THEM YOU HAVE A "MIND BLOWING PROMO PRICE" IMMEDIATELY AFTER SHIPPING. Their obvious question would be, "Why didn't you offer that promotion previously?" There's no good answer.

3. DON'T SEND THE BUYER GIFTS. Don't send them Starbucks gift cards and other prepaid gift cards with the enclosed note saying, "Thanks so much for this order!" Some companies take it in a negative way. They don't want gifts. They're doing business with you because they like your brand and your product. The gift may be interpreted as a bribe or appreciation for a favor.

4. DO NOT GIVE OUT YOUR HOME NUMBER. Keep this

relationship on a strictly business level, especially at this beginning stage. The fact that the retailer liked your product doesn't give you the right to bug them on the weekend. No one likes to be called at four in the morning to discuss a business issue.

This last item brings us back to communication. It should be effective, appropriate, and professional. Along those lines, one important element of communication that is worth mentioning is that when you do receive the purchase order or any other documentation from the retailer, it's vital that you acknowledge that you have received it. Many companies will send notification emails that they have sent the order. When you confirm the nice response, they'll feel more comfortable working with you in the future.

Here is a sample reply message which you can make use of when you have received a notification message from your retailer:

"Thank you for your order. We received your purchase order # at (time and date). We will start production of your order within the next forty-eight to seventy-two hours. If there is any urgency on the order, feel free to contact us so that we can take the appropriate steps. Once your order is ready to ship, we will notify you via email with a tracking number and estimated delivery date. Thank you for your business. "

BUILDING EXCELLENT RELATIONSHIPS WITH RETAILERS

One thing that retailers love is a company with a well organized structure. If they perceive that you have created a simple organization with a simple process, they will be eager to work with you. Keeping things simple shows your expertise and indicates that you will not give them hassles. When you ship your products quickly and efficiently, they will want to work with your brand.

One of the worst things that you can do to your business is to make it overly complicated. Some brands have unique products to offer that will never go global because of these issues. For instance, if you, as a producer, have wonderful products but possess a bad communication culture, do you think that retailers will be willing to build a long-term relationship with you? The answer is obvious: No retailer wants to work with your brand if they realize that it will take a lot of work and potentially cost them time and money. The question to answer now is, how do you simplify and streamline your business process?

There are several ways to approach this. One important way to demonstrate that you are in control of your process is rigorous record-keeping. Big-time retailers look out for small businesses that know how to maintain airtight records of all of their business transactions. Professional record-keeping sends the message that you pay attention to details. The big retailers do not want to work with small-time producers that are so haphazard in their approaches to business; retailers believe they might forget the details of the deals that they signed. Retailers are not impressed by producers that come in later asking for something different than what was outlined in the agreed-upon document.

Another way to demonstrate to your clients that you are on top of things is a shipping process that is simple and manageable. Making mistakes in your first order shipped is a very bad sign. If your process is too complicated for you to handle, making it difficult to ensure proper labeling, the big retailers might regard the relationship with you too burdensome. You may have a superb product, but if your shipping process is nonsense, that product will not go global.

Not everyone will earn their Retail PhD—especially if they aren't privy to the secrets we share here in this book. But you now have your diploma in hand, and you're ready to take on the retail world. And we'll be right here with you, every step of the way, if you need us.

CONCLUSION

We covered a lot of ground here, didn't we? By now, you should have all the tips and checklists you need to get your products into retail stores. But checklists aren't all you'll need as you navigate the retail brick-and-mortar world. If you finish this book with only those checklists in hand, then you'll have missed the most important points.

Those points aren't tangible, either—much like the power of a brand. You could have all the physical equipment you need to move forward in the retail world, but if you're missing the confidence, the knowledge, and the ability to handle the inevitable rejections, you still have a long path to success.

Your very first lesson is to believe in yourself, your product, and your vision. If you don't believe yourself, no one else will. Your story won't resonate with buyers or retailers.

Which begs the question: What is the story we are telling?

Simply put, it is the story of your business journey. This story is your past, present and future. Perhaps some of the journey hasn't been written for you yet, but it's all there in the preceding chapters waiting to unfold. In this, our final chapter, we'll pull all of the pieces of this story together.

The world of business has changed over the years. Product making and purchasing are just the tip of the iceberg. Businesses must now concern themselves with building brands.

Your path to success is a series of impressions. Impressions that you make on retailers, consumers—everyone who interacts with you or your product. Let's be clear: it all proceeds from the product. If you're building the story of your brand, it begins with a compelling product. But you're not merely selling your product as you build your business. As we stressed early on, you're selling your brand.

And remember: You only have so much control over your brand. In the end, your customers will determine whether or not you kept your promises.

The net effect of these interactions, these chances to tell your story, is the brand identity you're building. You may control your particular vision of that identity, how you want that story to exist in the minds of consumers as they see your product on the shelf. You control it through every interaction and as you follow the steps we've clearly outlined in this book. If—and only *if*—you keep every promise, then you can also control public perception of your brand. The story your buyers hear will be the story you've told from the beginning.

The world is filled with success stories of people who

understood the secrets outlined in this book. Some learned them from us, as we will discuss shortly, and others learned them from other sources or stumbled upon them, but the important thing is that the template for success is backed up by countless examples.

A SUCCESS STORY

They're everywhere. These success stories can be found on the shelves of retailers across the country. So many success stories repeat the same template. One such story is a specialty baking mix company that worked with us to expand their operations.

These specialty mixes were for items such as brownies, cornbread, cookies, and banana bread. The founder was initially inspired by a mix that her parents picked up on a trip. It was very simple, only requiring the addition of a single ingredient. Suddenly, the wheels started turning and the owner began to conceptualize her vision for her product. She had worked in the lucrative but stressful world of Hollywood public relations. Within a month of her product epiphany, she quit her day job and began preparing her products.

Her initial vision was strong. Once she settled on her inspiration, she was willing to upend her life to pursue it. No, this is not something that everyone can practically afford to do, but everyone can learn from her confidence. From the beginning, she had vision and belief—two key ingredients for retail-ready success.

Once devoted full time to fulfilling her vision, the founder rented space in a commercial kitchen each night, preparing mixes from her prototypes. Her mother helped package the mixes in the dining room in boxes her father, who worked in marketing, had envisioned.

The first step toward market penetration was a small chain of grocery stores specializing in natural foods: New Leaf Community Markets. By doing this, she was in alignment with one of our most important suggestions: it's smart to start small and build. She did.

Within a short time, this niche company had grown and was picked up by Whole Foods stores at over seventy locations. It was a logical progression, from the small single location of a natural foods grocer to a larger reach within the same market.

Today, the founder has a larger operation. The mixes are made by employees in a commercial kitchen. Packaging takes place in a warehouse. Her mixes now occupy spaces on shelves in over a thousand stores nationwide. She did all of this without any outside investors, by following a clear vision and taking sensible and professional steps towards growth and branding exactly like the ones outlined in this book. The title of this book refers to "Retail-Ready Secrets," but we're letting the secret out. Our goal is to share this information to empower small business owners across the country.

OUR VISION

For a long time now, we have worked behind the scenes to help some of the largest brick-and-mortar retailers grow. As we said in the dedication, we are where we are because of our fathers, who not only shared their knowledge of entrepreneurship with us but also passed along their spirit of generosity.

Our goal with this book has been to reveal our secret retail ready business strategies that we have used for many decades, secrets we learned from our fathers and many others who went before. These strategies allow small entrepreneurs to play in the same field with the big businesses. It has helped us in our business and with our brands. We're in the perfect position to give back and help others grow in the same way.

Our mission is to share our knowledge with business owners, helping them scale their business to the next level regardless of their industry and fierce competition. We show you how to use physical products to build a strong powerful brand and make a bigger impact, even if you are new to products. For decades, we have worked with some of the largest retailers in the world who kept the power of private label branded products to themselves.

Later, we began to work with smaller businesses, helping their brands skyrocket and sell in some of the biggest stores in the world to achieve a global impact. From there, we began sharing our secrets and the power of physical products. We have had the honor of spreading this unique secret to more than eleven-thousand students, providing vibrant opportunities to establish their businesses with major retailers.

We thank you for reading along and supporting our mission. If you felt you gained value from this book, please tell others it. We encourage you to share our strategies with other business owners. We need to band together, help each other, and support each other. Together let's level the playing field and share the success. Let us support you on this fantastic retail journey. You can find us over at priavtelabeluniversity.com and on Facebook to find more tips and updates! Join our community of likeminded businesses.

We want to leave you with this last thought: At the opening of this chapter, we said that our goal was to help you tell the story of your business's success. Imagine knowing what you know now, how it will dictate your success for tomorrow. You have the tools to make today the day your retail success story begins. You have an incredible private label product, the blueprint to make it retail ready, the confidence to strive, and the vision to get you there. Are you up for the ride? You are ready! You are Retail Ready! Your success story is ready to be written.

And we can not wait to hear all about it!

ABOUT THE AUTHORS

In 1983, Neil Gwartzman dove into the private labeling industry when he joined his father's wildly successful, brick-and-mortar manufacturing and importing company. After learning the business from the ground up, he committed himself to distill everything he and his father knew into a step-by-step system that could be used to easily and consistently identify, source and private label products for any company in any industry.

Over the years, Neil has worked with some of the biggest chain stores in the world, and has also private labeled over 800 products that have sold in more than 600 retail stores.

Neil taught the system to Karen in 2004, when she was a dental hygienist looking for ways to make extra money. Revenue from her new private label business quickly eclipsed her meager salary, making it an easy decision to quit the dental industry. She joined Neil in his mission to help entrepreneurs and business owners leverage private label products – once a strategy available only to retail giants – to scale their companies and increase brand recognition.

Karen and Neil **still use this finely tuned system every single day – with clients and with their private label products.**

At Private Label University, Karen and Neil know the hidden secrets of how to find the perfect product for your business... create it (the right way) for you and your clients... and get it on the right platform to reach up to 600x more clients than you are reaching now. They've also tested and identified the **key steps required to sell millions of dollars in private label products** on your own website, on Amazon and other online marketplaces, as well as in retail.

Learn more and get support in their private Facebook group: facebook.com/groups/PrivateLabelUniversity/.

f facebook.com/PrivateLabelUniversity

Checklist

1. Product purchased at the lowest possible price from the manufacturer.
2. Production volumes and shipping fast and effective (no hold ups).
3. Packaging retail ready for the specific stores you pitch to.
4. Line sheet completed.
5. Terms and conditions and contracts.
6. Advertising strategy budget in place.
7. Verbal pitch perfected.
8. Shipping and logistics set.
9. Discount and rebate structure in place.
10. List of retailers perfect for your product.

Notes:

CHECKLIST

1. HAVE YOU DONE YOUR RESEARCH? Do your
   schoolwork! Visit and understand the stores you
   need to be in (or if nothing else, look at their
   website) and see what makes that retailer the right
   place for your product and brand before reaching
   out to the buyer.

2. IS YOUR PRESENTATION RETAIL-READY? Is your
   packaging correct for the type of retailer you are
   pitching to? Do you have the right legal information
   and testing done for that market?

3. DO YOU HAVE A STORY AND VISION BEHIND YOUR
   BRAND? Buyers need to associate with the
   individual or business behind the brand and hear
   your story.

4. ARE YOUR WEBSITE AND SOCIAL MEDIA PLATFORMS
   PROFESSIONAL? The first thing a buyer will do is
   Google your website and check out what people are
   saying about your brand. Make sure your online
   collateral expresses your brand and highlights your
   products. Your essence on the web will show the
   buyer that you pay attention to your business. It's
   also a great way for buyers to see what you can
   offer before meeting with you.

5. DO YOU HAVE A LINE SHEET OR SALES SHEET? Buyers

are constantly inundated with product entries. Stand out from the group by having a line sheet that includes all the crucial information that buyers need to compose a buy request: costs and pricing, SRP, SKUs, barcodes, discounts, terms and conditions, shipping, and MOQ.

6. Do you know your competition? Determine who your competitors are, so you can speak confidently about what makes your line different, and how it fills a void in the market. You can throw in stats and numbers that impress.

7. Do you have a powerful pitch rehearsed and ready? You can't wing it, not with so much riding on your successful pitch.

8. Do you have samples? If you are meeting face to face samples are mandatory.

9. Have you considered marketing? Stores need to know that you are doing your part in getting the word out about your brand. Past sales, reviews, and testimonials are so important to share with the buyer. They want to know you will support them in getting traffic into their stores, so share your plan.

10. Are you confident? You must walk in with your head high and share your love of your brand and product. Help the buyers to fall in love, too.

NOTES

NOTES